Try

Winner

of the

Iowa Poetry

Prize

Try

Poems by

Cole Swensen

University of Iowa Press

Iowa City

University of Iowa Press, Iowa City 52242
Printed in the United States of America
http://www.uiowa.edu/~uipress
Printed on acid-free paper
Library of Congress Cataloging-in-Publication Data
Swensen, Cole, 1955–

    Try: poems / by Cole Swensen.

      p.   cm. — (Iowa poetry prize)

    ISBN 0-87745-659-3 (pbk.)

    I. Title. II. Series.

    PS3569.W384T79   1999

    811'.54—dc21   98-47408

04   05   06   07   08   P   5   4   3   2

TO PETER

Contents

Acknowledgments

My thanks to the following journals in which some
of these pieces first appeared:

American Letters and Commentary: "Trio"

Colorado Review: "Whatever Happened to Their Eyes,"
   "*Auguste Rodin*, THE KISS," and "*Chantal Akerman*, THE EAST"

Common Knowledge: "There"

Fourteen Hills: "Triarchy"

New American Writing: "Triad" and "Trine"

Psalm: "Triune"

Rhizome: "Éventail"

Prologue

Whatever Happened to Their Eyes

Throughout the history of painting
Risen until caught in rising. Arrested.
Even stunned and so for a moment
stilled and toward
                      My angel of Giotto, MADONNA
OGNISSANTI, *1310*: the right eye
traveling, planned, fled and
the left fixing forward like a pin.
He who watches him who wings
world without end and where
were you when she spun around and stared
and my God what on earth
has happened to their eyes?

Andrea di Cione, called Orcagna, STROZZI ALTARPIECE, *1354–57*: The plague
has passed but leaving any eye at the center of a painting drilling, stopped in
shock from all moving but forward to where a body barely now is standing:
viewer hold me to you, lace this fracture to a future
lace this
lace which
is mostly empty space seems to hold the very air in place.

Girolamo di Benvenuto, THE JUDGMENT OF PARIS, *c. 1500*: Two looking
down, one looking up, all weight there concentrated. What labor to glance
and hauling home these seeing stones and Mary Magdalena dressed in red
nearly turns around. There's an eye there but barely where it waits for the
dead with their peculiar sight wedded until bone.

Peculiar and remember.

                      Face that came undone.

Andrea Mantegna, Mars and Venus, *known as* Parnassus, *c. 1495*: Every
woman's eye has started to glide or trip toward
heaven and earth or dive
and come to see: all five flights will fail you
for the ear is such a little cup, the smell, the taste, the touch, not won
and the horses winged.

What they saw. For to see

is to see everything. Inverted sky. Inveterate spy. From late medieval times
through the Renaissance, one loaded site drives down to a point, and one
could say no it is the face surrounding but and though the mouth, but no
you're lying:
I saw someone leaving
and I saw the world, which was meant only for background, come to life.

(*Giovanni Bellini* your Christ Blessing, climbing eye over eye some inside
stair, a spiral that raises two fingers, one hand, heading toward heaven with a
hole in it and a hole in the other one: twinned sun and absence see
the phrase "the sight of blood" could mean something utterly else
and saw that it was
and made the body clay made the body, from the eyes down, fall away in
sheets.

and I saw someone leave and I saw the world that thrives on light clench and
cleave.

Triad

Noli Me Tangere, *Unknown Spanish Painter,*
early fourteenth century

1

Should the painter be distracted, should some sharp noise alarm him or pass-ing thought disarm. All the saints in their flaming skins. And at first glance seem to have an extra finger.

2

Note the grace entirely based on precise. Sudden ballet as you back away from
the depicted: Story One: If you touch
the sky will turn blue
                    (of our child
            to the tips of the fingers
      to the ceiling suddenly
                to the sight   so   Story Two:

If you profane   this is not flesh   with your supple
seething soon to be saintly and I

with a lock on the body and the sunlight cutting straight through me and I

picked up a brush and what's breathing
is not necessarily living

not that I have left but leave my

in your moth-fingered hands, in your million-fingered hands, a third story:
Now everything is sky and
where the body joins the body
a flickering solidity
encounters the returning
touch finding a different erring
and recognizing the difference,
which is how hands are formed and then lives:
miles sewn back on each other and the seam
some secret plenty.

3

When the sky was still gold

Mary Mary quite so many
to be reaching and always
toward that receding
land and body: body of clay
and a landscape made of faces.
Grace us in our unraveling flesh;
one alone must stay on earth
and I loved you so that I insisted:
Distill it. I, who can never be
single, splayed through a chiseled bevel
into the blues and greens and she's
wearing red, which is why she
gets the breadth, thus does not end.

Trilogy

One

1

The guard peers closely
at the painting. Count.

The fingers. The figures. The
strange sweep from waist

to chest to head. His hand reaches out
within a second of

2

She sweeps upward. Up
to where the gold sky might

What would the touch
if it did not first

run up against
a man who is in the end a man

3

She touched the painting
as soon as the guard

turned his back. Respond.
I said turn around. I

screamed, I drowned, I
thought you were home.

I touched the surface of the canvas.
It was I, the sound of salt. And fell
and is still falling through a silent earth.

Two

1

A deep red in the sky that has nothing
to do with the season but quiets

Outside drinking coffee and wine and watching.
Look, he's speaking, leaning over to his neighbor.

Look how the lines around his eyes and mouth.
Fleet. Part. What of that. Replies.

2

She crosses the square in a bright red coat.
Look how they look at her, look up

from their talking. There is no thought
here of leaving. There is no thought.

There are people crossing the square
arm in arm, in threes and fours and alone in great numbers.

3

Joseph Albers, THE INTERACTION OF COLOR, *1975*. I've heard
that no one is ever repeated or ever precisely named.

She took the coat off the peg.
Even to herself, she said it was her own.

She crosses the square on her way home.
She will not stop at a café, she will not talk, she will just go home.

Three

1

The minute progressions between grey and black
becoming one against the red that stares back.

Because she knows they are watching, she will not turn around.
Home is a sound repeated to solid, to something that will hold.

Look, there goes a man with his left hand left lightly
on the head of his child. There they go.

2

In the painting, all the reaching hands are growing.
In the gallery, everything was green and gold and red

Made the sun, though deep, cut through:
Within the door was a window; within the window, a jar.

Inside the jar, carefully there, the love need not be
assigned in order to fix and ignite.

3

She had to cross the square in order to get home.
She was one. And one by one, they looked up and watched.

When the guard turned around, the gesture was gone.
A woman stood back and said no.

She stood back, looking at the painting and said isn't it fine
that a woman wearing red could arrive at a gold sky. Remind.
Or else in falling. And nothing broke. The rift
shifts open the devout. A finger that exceeded number, a
fingertip.

Triune

after three paintings by Olivier Debré

Liberty

to C.

Person, pale, female
In green there is

and moves and lives and

Thirsty, she picked up
the empty cup and left the room.

Two people on a bench.
A tall person standing.
I couldn't help it,
to have not done so would have
rendered me inhuman.

The pale green makes the woman
seem freer than the rest of us.

Inside her is a blue egg.
She lives with it,
which is why she looks like that:

No one has wings.
No one lies.

Liberty

to H.

Garden of red.

You see him bend down
to pick up something small.
He's a small man with gloved hands.

Holy on
We're bound for all

A sense of the chest
opening and opening again.

They have to break the ribs
to get to the heart in time.

A single man shrinks in the light.
All that fits in the average palm.

His sense of color drowns the eye. He is not crying.
No one lies.

Liberty

to E.

Deep deepening of the Loire.

You can keep on joining.
You can join for years.

The natural extension of the hand
is the world is
reflected in its
proper motion here

is something you forgot; put it
in your pocket; touch it
to return, once, twice

Three children stand on the bank of a stream
throwing stones, laughing, jostling.
Look, their shadows flick through the water like fish
free of their bodies.

Trio

after the work of Hieronymus Bosch

Here

By the time we got there we were already alive, but what exactly did that look like and who exactly was looking. It's a matter of what the thinking, throughout its enormous building, considered thought and how it worked its way through the blood. Such as: There was a castle here once, built right there where that tree now stands with your arms out, with your head held high, and the flaming spear caught in the topmost branch caused the fire. A million people died or will die of similar affections, carrying home the bricks and the beams, one by one, the history is reassembling what you once said: we got here in time so it is you and I who this time will live.

Here

When the castle burned, the whole sky caught fire, a sheer red dome and we all stopped a moment, looked up from our work, and when the world burned down and made the ocean into a window, and all that life was beautiful to see streaming through its million greens in layer after layer, and we all pointed and marveled and promised to come back one day when we could stay awhile and whisper what we really want is the working one, the one with all the gears and parts that move, the bodies that breathe, the matter that touches the way we'd been taught to touch, just lightly while drawing in breath, letting the other one drift around inside a bit where the cells open out and, in opening, renounce the gift of a single body, the graft of a private history, the tip of a foot that won't sink back into the painting.

Deictic

World on its own. No one, none, not fused to the wall of the vein or is the vein itself. An absolute motion, now we are going. Look at us leaving and leaving nothing behind. A whole civilization once vanished from this very spot without a scratch. So you can be here now and be it at the same time and you can take it with you and when you're gone, so will be my eyes replaced by eyes. I smile with a certain amnesia, an amnesia that knows itself certainly, certainly they all lived here once and they were beautiful then but only then.

Triptych

The Flight into Egypt

Reach me to
      new all other
      land
That flees
Known. Recognized though
you can't remember what
the house looks like it's huge

And carried in her arms
and in her arms held
             and stopped a moment to sit

where the cells coalesce
exchange address
          though it's huge

and does not walk alone.

"From the fourteenth to eighteenth centuries, we find in the painterly obses-
sion with the Flight into Egypt a recognition of . . . as being . . . who focus . . .
here on earth, though without . . . and the function of the metaphor (Fly! Fly!)
in setting the stage for the nineteenth-century fabrication of Orientalism."

To Egypt I will go
with a penny in my hand
and a song in my heart
there to start
a new land
and cover it with snow

alone
palms down
there in the spare
and the sun
there the going on   one runs toward
turns huge   and found

                                        looking closely at the background land-
scapes, that the holy family enters not a heavenly but a very worldly world, a
world just like ours except that it's not and that it can't be reached.

When the angel came to Joseph in a dream and said

(Rembrandt, 1627)

These are my people, my mountains, my flesh
and under cover of night
you will learn how to fly

and fled.

Hans Memling, 1435–1494: Mary in marine, Cobalt Mary from the bottom of the sea and uncommonly at peace while Joseph in the background picks dates from a palm while in the background the world grows more lush, a lake, a road, horsemen in the field of a prosperous farm just below the trees along the skyline in lace, and another house and it goes on and on like this.

For every male infant under
leave this world but one behind
and behind the glorious city
running as in water to another
you will hear a slight click
as you cross over
and so the child will live.

And so Mary took into her hand
And so the child, though sleeping, saw
And so Joseph prayed, stooped and prayed

Poussin: the angel is still there but Joseph looks back at her in fear while Mary simply looks back and the child, simply, at us. Behind it all, an impossibly intricate world that turns the sun blue.

by heart and yet knew the way and went
out walking quite early this morning
and went on
and will cross a great
will have at your back
                              voice, coin, seal
and never leave your side

Someone is looking now at the painting, thinking Mary, that your back looks just a little tired, the shoulder inclined to the right, the child forever asleep, and stopped on the way to Egypt and flies.

Jacopo Robusti, called Tintoretto, 1518–1584:
a farming scene at peace and in
the right background, everyone heading
into the picture while the holy family heads out, heads on, runs into us in an exile of flesh. And of what was left in the living world.

And so Herod sent his men
and in the background now we see

Face on fire that refuses flame.

extracts the light, divides the remainder by

a single line wraps the day
in a strand of sun that goes beyond what
but has yet been and yet and so

And so Herod sent his men
to follow in
and impervious to rain and wind
as if by accident
you get used to these things

Pierre Patel called le père, 1673, LE REPOS PENDANT: The classical age re-gained and incidentally within, a little holy family so small you almost over-look the bird paused on Joseph's hand as he watches the boy who reaches for the open wings.

blue for the world that never touches ground; red for the living who love living and thus live on

They have stopped
on the way to Egypt
balanced between and they went

blue for the world beyond; red for the woman who drowns

not quite singing but humming while they listened
for the hooves of all those horsemen only one escaped
as he heard a slight click and the scent of something tropical

arose from her hair. Mary Mary quite please hurry some faces grow calmer
at the sight

Elsheimer, 1603, dead in Rome by 1610, "carried them as near to the limits of truth as such subjects can go without entirely" Dear, they could be camping; darling, please pass me the salt, I feel a sudden weight, a preponderance of light when I have never been the sort to fly in my dreams.

Claude Lorrain, a simple picnic under trees.

And so we come to the miracle of the wheat.

And so Mary begged the plowman: say you saw us as you sowed
And in the background something turned
the sun blue and the city sank
and if your feet leave the ground, know the child will live. You will hear a slight
click and the wheat will shoot up five feet in a single night and there you hid
while Herod's men thought of other years, of bread that grows, of picnics and
houses and music made huge. Dream on. An angel chases you through a world
turned gold and of the woven sword
the definitive word
and all the children dead back there and
of wheat that flies to Egypt below a green sun.

And so an angel flew to Egypt
and there we were.
Joseph said
stop here
(my dear, you look a little tired).

There

"an implicit assumption that the concrete world is inaccessible"

"an implicit assumption that the concrete world is more lovable"

Love me and you love the world.
he said while over his shoulder
or through a little window just to the right
of the picture

blue and green
this haze will never falter

"Throughout the Middle Ages and for several centuries thereafter, the eye was
continually directed toward a scene of moving people, but
and in intricate detail
sometimes down to leaf by leaf
it's spring and a farmer
who shall remain nameless, no more than half an inch tall
plows a world we will not enter

Touch me and you touch the world because color is simple to fall in love with
a distance.

Backing up
Pulling in
It's the oldest form of protection.

and the world so easily broken.

LES AMOURS DISARMED ON EARTH, *Francesco Albani, 1620*: They are cutting the wings off the angels.

PLANE 1: People, often in action, often in contact: there a hand rests on an arm, there a foot steps on a robe or an eye touches your eye without blinking.
PLANE 2: A city; at the very least, manmade structures. The middle distance. Like you could go away without leaving.
PLANE 3: There is indeed the unspeakable, and it can't show itself; this is the real.

Sassetta, 1392–1450: What is that ark hovering
over the young-Saint-Francis-deciding? And what is that paw in your hand doing connected on the farther end to a (note the limbs in the background still bleeding) wolf?

"In these paintings in which all the people (always in the foreground) are not the point but come so far forward to mask, to shield

PLANE 1: The war goes on. Christ comes down. The Virgin chats with the Chancellor Rolin.
PLANE 2: So often it's only a window.
PLANE 3: Noli me tangere.

". . . who realized that the world could not be drawn closer than towns and men; that it would always recede, recoil from such assumption and in so doing and with flagrant glory, mock them."

wanted only to point out that the world is an impossible thing

to have never seen

that green now blue the folding

hands of a larger

and yet do live here

"is not of this world, but there is also something of the world that is not

So rarely in these paintings is anyone speaking.

Even *Joachim Patenier, 1480–1524*: as Saint Jerome nestles down in the desert:
1) The foreground, bleak; the living, beyond. Look, he's even brought his hat, broad-brimmed like a Sunday out and placed just so primly.
2) Count the buildings: 1, 2, 3.
3) Now it's in color.

(And everything that lives there an unrefracted white: farmer, sheep, oxen, goat on the edge of a cliff, three birds just taking off.)

Land becomes art through applied joy and shock.

Antonello da Messina: Now Jerome among arches and angles while the world pours in through the windows, lions, birds

architectural weather; the spherical gesture of an uncontrollable sky.

MANNA FROM HEAVEN, *Master of the Manna, c. 1470*: Heaven can't be seen but the scene in which they stand or just beyond, a great around and moving out as long as—don't move, blink, or reach can be content or at least resolved will continue to unfurl.

"how often it is a river that leads our eye as viewers farther."

For Bellini so loved the world

There's a world out there that isn't there.

gathered all the pieces
and led them across the sky—
there's a stag, there's a bull, there
a tree on fire all the way home
built a house of them: one and
one and one what's done
is hardly done. *Chagall, 1917.*

Noli Me Tangere

I am a gardener
Here you see my spade
There you see my fields
Inside, the ice-clouds
row after
and now row
There is no river
They all lied
I am a gardener
And you can't touch me now.

Early illuminations, on the other hand, chose to keep the angels present.

Run and tell my mother
Whose flesh is water
That her flesh is water
Row

Le Parement de Narbonne, *1375*: Commissioned by Charles V. Whose
last image in an unrolling life featuring Christ after Christ after Christ in grey

on silk he reaches down as if to touch as she reaches up but all their hands, lost fans, fluttering like fins dying of fresh air.

NOLI ME TANGERE
or THE RESURRECTED CHRIST APPEARING TO MARY MAGDALENE, *Poussin*, painted for Jean Pointel in 1653. They could have been dancing or a single body as the line of the untouched hand extends exactly to where the heart should have been and the whole body also open but this is my spade and my eternal future while you will kneel much longer with arms outstretched and that open place that used to be your chest heading inward.

Whose flesh is water
Know
Below the face
A stroke more certain
A line of demarcation and
Another face goes on

To one of permanent touch

To recognize the rest

the line between flesh
and everything flesh
grew lonely and its own
Keep on
coming down
to earth in little pieces.

Also in the Prado, *Le Corrège*. Here Christ is more beautiful and only the handle of his spade can be seen. It could be the handle of anything, and Mary, too, leaning toward the real.

Go and tell my mother
it's the water of the flesh
that rises unto heaven
drop by drop there was nothing left to cancel
it starts just below the skin
and then can't stop beginning.
Mary who remembers, who sees her face in rivers,
raise your head a little higher;
the vase on the window sill has fallen, and it was I who grew those flowers
once when I was human I
thought I saw something beautiful. What
do you think you're doing
with those arms

Fra Angelico, 1387–1455, left the gold behind and now the sky is full of sky

that I was living as surely as now I'm rising
with a world behind but lying: it was as close as you can get to a body
and what do you think you're doing—
River before and river thereafter
Once wheat grew in a single day
and I was running as now I'm running as something odd is falling but
upward and you must have heard
and now must run and tell my brothers "once
he had ends to his fingers

"As early as the thirteenth century, we see her in red on gold on wood on her knees and already her hand is reaching and already the fire has reached her brain without burning."

A little click

and there stood
beyond touch
cannot be a body but must carry

a little fire that catches on
a vagrant thread a whole field
in bloom
and thus what
heard

Yet you could turn to me
and yet not see
what face has now and what has the world
grown perfect in its blues and greens
and can't be touched or reached what town
we could have been
dancing. What did and what
was that little click
I heard when you turned
with the angels and stared

(Sometimes I lean down and, with two fingers only, touch the top of your head, which makes you carry a skull through the rest of the history of painting.)

Rembrandt, 1651: the darkness all around them they are finally alone.

"reveals an obsession with the triumph of light over darkness"

"here reaches his ultimate expression of the eternal triumph"

"finally triumphs over the limitations of two dimensions"

and bloomed in storm
and was not the tomb but in the hand, the earth
overturned: earned. This is what it cost: a simple gasp,
a little lust, said

I, the one who grew this that
became my body
no it couldn't have been I who was speaking
repeat after me

Angelo di Cosimo called Bronzino, 1561: what can they have to say to each other
now do not touch that which your right hand almost touches, almost absent

every hand (from the left of the frame) that the picture contains (someone is
calling me), raised or in the process of rising.

Once I saw something beautiful   has seen and has known
                                     will not relinquish the body

will unbury

below the bone
Sainte-tous Marie I never thought it simple to be seen.

And so her tears fell onto burning soil and her dress turned red and her body
fell down like a body

picks up his spade and starts digging

Mary Mary quite only my only you have no idea what it is to touch.

And I too asked why are you crying
"Rabbouni" and fell into a garden; go
and tell the others that whatever grows does so forever

William Etty, 1787–1849. This time it's Christ who wears red and the angels
laugh and the soldier dies.

Le Baroche, 1526–1612. Mary pulls back astonished and it is Jesus, so hand-
some, who holds out his hand but still must say, "Don't

Anonymous Chinese painter, eighteenth century. Mary just turns her back on
    him and cries.

and rose to ask
what disturbed
and deep mistrust
must run the flesh
of a woman with such
stunning face. You must
not touch.

Titian, 1488–1567. Against the background of a spherical world, and thus and
does and is no end.

Triarchy

Narrative in Pieces

Story One

CALVARY, *Master of the Death of Saint Nicholas of Munster,*
second half of the fifteenth century

Center stage, foregrounded: Christ
in the act of being pierced
in the breast while the V. Mary swoons and Mary M. looks on and in the
distance on another hill, another central figure
is being taken down (deposing from his cross) what is (was)
lost in that shift and again at his feet
yet another figure,
identically dead, now is held
in three women's arms and just below them, three women are laying
another figure into a pale stone tomb. Look how all
their wounds know exactly where to go and below,
running like a prédelle along the frame,
a catalogue of all the wildflowers that were that week in bloom.

Story Two

ALTARPIECE OF THE DEPOSITION OF CHRIST,
Joos van Cleve, 1520–1525

Same Mary M. as the so lovely one in the P. of the Legion of H., S.F., and
again narrative by repetition: in the background we see
something going on in a womb-like tomb while in the foreground
he has just come down and Mary's hands are doing
that strange flexing thing—fingers
flying apart and up and out and yet they stay bound
to their stumps, which are stumps. In the foreground
a bronze bowl full of blood and a sponge.

Story Three

SAINT JOHN IN THE WILDERNESS, *Giovanni di Paolo,*
mid fifteenth century

Saint John in the living
the wilderness in the sea
in the grey-green space of pink cities the size of thumbs. One: leaving the hut,
open out, point the toe. The house shrinks back into itself. The house slips off
and (two:) Saint John going on to his blue land, crosses, crossings, crossing
over to what strewn among the rearing mountains, the here now there in the
wilderness of palms and perfectly plowed fields grows and over the hill.

                    What light gait.

                             What shall give

     thus live   on
                    we

                             reside
                             we
                             realign

       we have no back.

Trinity

Auguste Rodin, CHRIST AND THE MAGDALENE, *1894*

Cross the body across the body.
The letters of the body
blend to a single body, a when
we were still living

to be carried on thereafter
Mary bury here your every

and so she laid
her face in the grave and
watched it fill with its own

and was replaced
though not perceived. Ghost of grace levied against sight
and is thus lost: if you

bend at the waist
ninety degrees to the right, then stretch
your left arm out, making
another right angle at the elbow
in order to reach the round of his shoulder,
the cross will not be broken but
will be multiplied against
the cross of his body broken at
the neck by a right angle to the spine
in order to lay a cheek against
her shoulder. Naked Mary chest to chest,
inside grief is a growing stone
that grows white and to look
like you never looked: asleep
and the peace on his face, sleeping.

Auguste Rodin, Christ and the Magdalene, *1894*

Two bodies on a cross and
neither forms a cross but
complicates the innate form
of the human frame to ascend
you must be made of stone

and you must cave in
from the breastbone and move on
through. Exchange. What is
in that little jar
where ends
what world;
Any life has so few friends
gone white on the way to our ghosts
and the jar sheds light
in some other room

we're alone
sleeping among statues in bronze and clay and well-dressed bone
It was a fragile sound;
who listened and thus must
beyond and drowned.

Auguste Rodin, CHRIST AND THE MAGDALENE, *1894*

Her hand though it reaches up
doesn't touch his shoulder
but lands beyond in a niche of rock
which is not rock, but plaster
on its way to bronze.
Neither got home.
Neither got found.
Her fingers caught
His arms encased
She's given up her legs,
her face, and now joined at the heart
which her halved body wholly hides:
this no, this love gone white and gone.

Trine

Cove

Covey of might

do convey
to my   my most
honor here what not only may
but will
                    that hearts a word

that flight (along the river as well as within the river, migration of dimension;
entire nation as a narrow line that stretches for miles and above, the hovering
dust of what dissolves the city into pieces so small they pass through a salt
shaker, a flour sifter, a human eye by the hundreds moving as a single gesture
down to the smallest finger in which the muscles are nonetheless meticulously
stitched to a longer anger: There is a body in the river. Carried light as
weather. Could not be identified but almost.)
                            my most
distinguished
must
the curving line
        carve
from simple fingers   friend
of a friend to find
within the hand
                    a thousand barely birds
        words for water
and a fire in the harbor. They're flying

(though they is always someone else and in some other country where the
thriving revolt.)

It is with great
and please believe
in my   may this
find you alive.

Dove

Dives, flock after flock

so convened. What lost
to each
                    signed,

I beg the pleasure of
and so won this only

measurement of an artery
when and ever shall be
multiple aviary
one less ceiling
one less boat   do send my most

(however lost can only be spoken. It's just a way of speaking. It's not the
mouth, but the throat that determines the limits of the vowels. Otherwise the
body carries on for years and years later the body in the river becomes thou-
sands, each thinking I should have lowered my eyes, I should have scarred my
face, I should have torn out my hair, I should have lied.)

without end and when

the thousandth one turned
and then they will

                              all those faces, eyes
and eyes
of my eternal gratitude   I find

(I died in a river but I did not drown, no not I says the body floating says the boat whose leaving came along and then stayed and then kept on staying.)
                         one less army
one more throat   to whom it may
it is with great
that I   and will and am
my only   and my always
then.

Woven

Strove the uncommon
                    unto custom

Thriving seemed
                            and then arrived
as the thread pulled
and the needle screamed
            friend
                        is searing skin
and then received

one more only
                    how oddly
any
            without end
walked all the way to the sea
Entire
                                    Please

and that I must

people clustered around fires
(and the harbor still on fire)
may I introduce

(what object with the object of holding was the hand and why does closing
the eyes make the edges more precise. You were born without a face. Stay.
I'm coming to. This which disperses. Names were not entered. Lists were not
made. No one was notified, which is what is meant by why does)

                        took shelter in
invented an

(a lie save only what in any case could not have been altered.)

Triage

Éventail

Tree of a thousand fans. The unphalanged hand. The mastery of wind in that one rows and below ground where the mirror image plows, Mary of Cleaves still believes it can restore; born with a malformed paw, unobstructed furl. The ginkgo dates from the world's second age. Nothing's changed. The veins arranged as a single sheet so uncontained on anything floats. Can shimmer, flicker through the unbounded thought thinking out abnormalities of growth and simply stayed aloft, arched out across ground zero in Nagasaki across the alleys of human shadows gilding the walls.

"They couldn't control the sky."

FAN: LANDSCAPE AFTER CÉZANNE, *Paul Gauguin, 1885*
It's the season in the shape,
the curve that comes down
to the brow and borrowed
from an orient and drowned.

Auguste Rodin, THE KISS, 1886–98

Taking them from the unfinished *Gates of Hell*, he executed three in marble
each nine feet tall, identical and entwined
in two bodies that break down to a
single point that lips. Which makes the bodies drape. Fall away
in sheets. Repeat. The three
aligned on a diagonal in a basement of the Gare d'Orsay.
They barely fit. Enumerate and yet
at no point could a viewer stand and catch
the echo of a single image splayed but other angles intervene.
One times three equals one. Toujours pour la
première fois etcetera. Give me your hands; they are cold to the touch and not
one but all and if nothing new under the sun we say slightly stunned who then
who, carved from the same score and different are
and a single lip
from four seals the refraction. A fan
is such a simple shape until it's a face until it's ours.

Even

This happened to a friend of mine, a very bright man, and it really did happen this way: he met a woman at a café or some equally casual place, and they'd hit it off, had gone out three or four times, and had gotten rather close, some warm embraces, kissed once or twice, and were getting nearer and nearer to a physical intimacy, so one day she said, there's something I think I should tell you; I have no left hand.

Epilogue

Chantal Akerman, THE EAST *(a documentary video), 1993*

What if she had not put the cellist so separately after the fifteen minutes of the camera's panning along the long line of human faces but had slowly over a ten-minute period brought the music up behind and faded the image of the single musician into and over the long line of human faces waiting for something in line side by side perhaps beside a train track so barely that it never quite arrived. What if all concerts were performed behind a huge screen onto which was projected a long line of faces all facing us and it had always been done this way. You can see hundreds, even thousands, of faces in fifteen minutes. It lets you lose track of the music.

THE IOWA POETRY PRIZE & EDWIN FORD PIPER POETRY AWARD WINNERS

1987
Elton Glaser, *Tropical Depressions*
Michael Pettit, *Cardinal Points*

1988
Bill Knott, *Outremer*
Mary Ruefle, *The Adamant*

1989
Conrad Hilberry, *Sorting the Smoke*
Terese Svoboda, *Laughing Africa*

1990
Philip Dacey,
    Night Shift at the Crucifix Factory
Lynda Hull, *Star Ledger*

1991
Greg Pape, *Sunflower Facing the Sun*
Walter Pavlich,
    Running near the End of the World

1992
Lola Haskins, *Hunger*
Katherine Soniat, *A Shared Life*

1993
Tom Andrews,
    The Hemophiliac's Motorcycle
Michael Heffernan, *Love's Answer*
John Wood, *In Primary Light*

1994
James McKean, *Tree of Heaven*
Bin Ramke,
    Massacre of the Innocents
Ed Roberson,
    Voices Cast Out to Talk Us In

1995
Ralph Burns, *Swamp Candles*
Maureen Seaton, *Furious Cooking*

1996
Pamela Alexander, *Inland*
Gary Gildner,
    The Bunker in the Parsley Fields
John Wood,
    The Gates of the Elect Kingdom

1997
Brendan Galvin, *Hotel Malabar*
Leslie Ullman, *Slow Work through Sand*

1998
Kathleen Peirce, *The Oval Hour*
Bin Ramke, *Wake*
Cole Swensen, *Try*